THE
TIMELESS
TEACHINGS
OF GURU ZUZU

AS TOLD TO TONY BROADBENT

FOR KIRK —
TO HELP INSPIRE FOND MEMORIES
OF BOB, AND RED, AND PHIL

7 MAY 2019 — Tony

New World Library
Novato, California

New World Library
14 Pamaron Way
Novato, California 94949

Design and interior text concept by Tony Broadbent
Illustration credits begin on page 120. Every effort has been made to contact original sources. If notified, the publishers of this book will be pleased to rectify an omission in future editions.

Library of Congress Cataloging-in-Publication Data

Names: Broadbent, Tony, author.
Title: The timeless teachings of Guru Zuzu / as told to Tony Broadbent.
Description: Novato, California : New World Library, [2019].
Identifiers: LCCN 2018053669 (print) | LCCN 2018055777 (ebook) | ISBN 9781608685943
    (e-book) | ISBN 9781608685936 (print : alk. paper) | ISBN 9781608685943 (ebook)
Subjects: LCSH: Cats--Anecdotes. | Cat owners--Anecdotes.
Classification: LCC SF445.5 (ebook) | LCC SF445.5 .B735 2019 (print) | DDC 636.8--dc23
LC record available at https://lccn.loc.gov/2018053669

First printing, May 2019
ISBN 978-1-60868-593-6
Ebook ISBN 978-1-60868-594-3
Printed in Canada

New World Library is proud to be a Gold Certified Environmentally Responsible Publisher. Publisher certification awarded by Green Press Initiative.

10   9   8   7   6   5   4   3   2   1

In memoriam
Joe and Marilyn
"Vernal Cats"
who first perceived
the wisdom of
Guru Zuzu

"When the student is ready,
the teacher will appear."
— Buddhist proverb

CONTENTS

ABOUT **GURU ZUZU**

SOMETIMES, SOMEONE COMES INTO YOUR LIFE AND YOU KNOW RIGHT AWAY THEY'RE MEANT TO BE THERE. IT'S AS IF THEY'RE A **CATALYST** FOR SOME CHANGE THAT'S ABOUT TO OCCUR IN YOUR LIFE.

IT COULD INVOLVE ANY ONE OF A THOUSAND THINGS: TO DO WITH **LOVE**, WITH OTHERS, EVEN WITH YOUR INNERMOST SELF.

SOMETIMES — AS FATE WILL HAVE IT — THOSE SPECIAL BEINGS THAT COME TO HELP US TURN OUT NOT TO BE HUMAN, BUT **FELINE**.

ONCE UPON A TIME, A LITTLE BLACK GREEN-EYED PUSSYCAT CAME INTO MY LIFE AND WAS ONE SUCH **WISE** BEING.

I CALLED HER **ZUZU** — AFTER "ZUZU'S PETALS" FROM FRANK CAPRA'S WONDROUS 1946 FANTASY FILM, *IT'S A WONDERFUL LIFE*, WHERE A LITTLE DAUGHTER'S GIFT OF ROSE PETALS BECOMES A REMINDER OF THE SANCTITY OF LIFE.

AS THE YEARS PASSED, ZUZU TAUGHT ME SO MANY WONDERFUL THINGS THAT I CAME TO THINK OF HER AS "THE **BLESSED** GURU ZUZU." I STILL DO.

EVEN THOUGH ZUZU'S NOW GONE FROM THIS WORLD, HER **GENTLE** WISDOM LIVES ON IN ME.

I HOPE THE SIMPLE IDEAS ABOUT LOVE AND LIFE AND FRIENDSHIP IN *THE TIMELESS TEACHINGS OF GURU ZUZU* — IN TURN — HELP INSPIRE YOU TO ENJOY THIS MOST WONDERFUL LIFE TO THE FULLEST.

ABOUT

YOU

SEARCH OUT
SPECIAL PLACES,
SAFE PLACES,
SECURE PLACES
TO BE ALONE IN,
AND YOU WILL
ALWAYS
FIND YOURSELF.

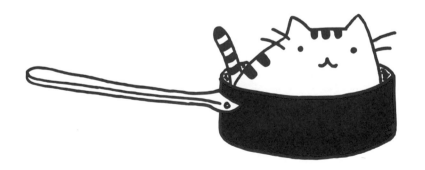

17

ALWAYS PAY
ATTENTION.
IT REPAYS
DIVIDENDS
IN MORE WAYS
THAN YOU
COULD EVER
IMAGINE.

JUST
BECAUSE
IT MOVES,
DOESN'T
NECESSARILY
MEAN THAT
IT'S **FOOD**
FOR YOU.

EVERYTHING

COMES

TO THOSE

WHO

PUT THEMSELVES

IN THE RIGHT

PLACE

AND **WAIT**.

23

HOW

YOU SEE

THE WORLD

DEFINES

WHAT

YOU

SAY **NO**

TO.

TAKE TIME
TO BE STILL,
TO BE QUIET,
SPHINX-LIKE,
AND LIFE
WILL OPEN UP TO YOU
IN MYRIAD
WAYS.

ALWAYS
BE PREPARED
TO FIGHT
FOR
WHAT
YOU **KNOW**
TO BE
RIGHT.

29

IF

YOU CAN

WALK WITH KINGS

AND NOT LOSE

THE COMMON TOUCH,

THE PATH

WILL ALWAYS **OPEN** UP

FOR YOU.

ALWAYS
REMEMBER,
NEVER LOSE
YOUR SENSE
OF **HUMOR**.
LIFE'S
FAR
TOO SHORT.

SOMETIMES,
IT BECOMES
CLEAR
YOU
SIMPLY
NEED TO
BELIEVE
IN YOU.

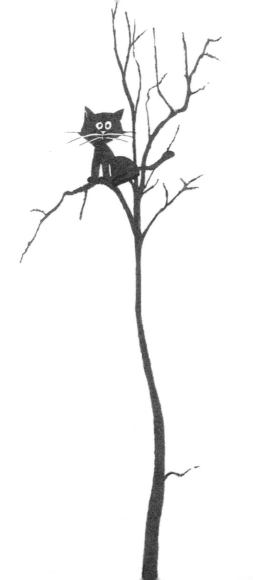

35

NEVER FORGET
WHO AND WHAT
YOU ARE,
AND THAT
YOU ALONE
ARE RESPONSIBLE
FOR WHAT IT IS
YOU **THINK** ABOUT.

I · AM · A · CAT

THE **WEAKNESS**
OF A KITTEN
IS STRONG
ENOUGH
TO BREAK
EVEN
THE STOUTEST
HEART.

39

ABOUT

LOVE

YOU CAN'T
ALWAYS GET
WHAT YOU WANT,
BUT GIVE
UNCONDITIONAL LOVE,
AND YOU VERY OFTEN
GET WHAT
YOU NEED.

43

GIVE
LOVE
TO GET
LOVE.
LOVE IS
ALWAYS
A TWO-WAY
STREET.

44

FIND OUT
WHAT
IT IS
YOU LOVE
DOING,
AND DO
A LOT
OF IT.

cat naps

LOVE
COMES
IN ALL SHAPES
AND SIZES
TO **FULFILL**
EVERY NEED,
WANT,
AND DESIRE.

49

SOMEDAY,
SOMEWHERE,
SOMEHOW,
YOU WILL
FIND
THE **PERFECT** MATCH
FOR YOUR
TYPE.

```
>   /\,,,,/ \
> > ( =';'= )
>   /*??*\
> (.|.|..|.|.)
```

TO BE
CONTENT
IS TO BE
GRANTED
A **BLESSING**
GREATER
THAN
RICHES.

53

ALL
LOVE
BEGINS
WITH
A HUGE
LEAP
OF
FAITH.

54

THE
LOVE
YOU MAKE
IS
EQUAL TO
THE
LOVE
YOU TAKE.

WANTED

DEAD AND ALIVE

SCHRÖDINGER'S CAT

LOVE

THE

ONE

YOU'RE

WITH

WITHOUT

CONDITIONS

OR RESERVATION.

LOVE
MEANS
UNDERSTANDING
THAT SOMETIMES
THE ONE
YOU LOVE
SIMPLY WANTS
TO BE **ALONE.**

LIFE

IS JUST A BOWL

OF CHERRIES.

SHARE

LIFE'S SWEETNESS

WITH

SOMEONE

YOU LOVE.

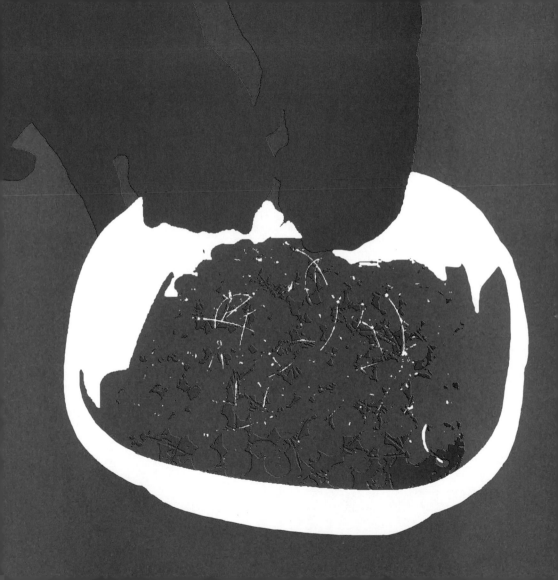

THERE'S
NO PLACE
IN
THE HUMAN **HEART**
THAT
A CAT
CANNOT
TOUCH.

ABOUT

OTHERS

WHEN
YOU MEET
A GOOD FRIEND,
SAY, "SO VERY GOOD
TO SEE YOU!
SO VERY **GLAD**
YOU'RE IN
MY LIFE."

69

DON'T ALWAYS
REVEAL
WHAT
YOU'RE THINKING.
A **SILENT**
STARE
SPEAKS
VOLUMES.

TIME

SPENT

WITH FRIENDS

AND **FAMILY**

IS ALWAYS

TIME

WELL

SPENT.

TAKE
ESPECIAL
COMFORT
IN
THE
KINDNESS
OF
STRANGERS.

75

GOOD
FRIENDS
COME
IN
ALL
SHAPES
AND
SIZES.

YOU DON'T
NEED
TO SCRATCH
PEOPLE.
MAKE YOUR MARK
IN OTHER,
MORE **AGREEABLE**
WAYS.

LET
BYGONES
BE
BYGONES.
NEVER
HOLD
A
GRUDGE.

81

IT'S GOOD
TO **CELEBRATE**
THE DANCE
OF LIFE
WITH
A CLOSE
CIRCLE
OF FRIENDS.

SOMETIMES,
SURPRISE A STRANGER
WITH THE WARMTH
OF YOUR GREETING.
IT CAN DO
NOTHING
BUT
DISARM THEM.

JUST
BECAUSE
YOU SEE **OTHERS**
DOING SOMETHING
DOESN'T
MEAN
YOU HAVE TO
DO IT TOO.

IT'S YOUR
DUTY
TO
PROTECT
OTHERS
WHO ARE NOT
AS STRONG
AS YOU ARE.

GIVE
FULL
EXPRESSION
TO YOUR JOY.
JOY
INCREASES
WHEN
IT'S SHARED.

ABOUT

LIFE

THERE ARE TIMES
WHEN YOU
NEED TO
SPEAK UP
TO ENSURE
THAT YOU
ARE
HEARD.

95

ONCE
THE OBJECTIVE
IS DEFINED,
CHANCE
FAVORS
THE
PREPARED
MIND.

IF IT DOESN'T
FEEL RIGHT...
SCOOT!
SCAT!
THEN TRY AGAIN
LATER.
TIMING
IS EVERYTHING.

DO
EVERYTHING
YOU DO
AS IF
IT'S THE ONLY THING
IN ALL THE WORLD
THAT TRULY
MATTERS.

100

YOU CAN

SIT

ON

THE FENCE

ONLY

FOR

SO

LONG.

DEEP THOUGHTS
CAN COME
TO YOU
IN THE VERY ODDEST
OF PLACES
IF YOU JUST
GIVE YOURSELF
TIME TO **THINK**.

BEFORE YOU **CLIMB**
TO EVEN GREATER
HEIGHTS,
IT'S WISE
TO KNOW
HOW TO GET
BACK DOWN
AGAIN.

BE

ESPECIALLY **ALERT**

AFTER NIGHTFALL,

AS ALL CATS

TEND TO

DISAPPEAR

IN

THE DARK.

TRAVERSEE DE CHATS

109

ENOUGH
IS
A FEAST.
THERE
IS
NO VALUE
IN
EXCESS.

110

111

WHEN
YOU NEED
TO VENT,
OR OFF-LOAD,
GO
DO IT
IN
PRIVATE.

THERE ARE TIMES
WHEN IT'S BEST
TO LET GO OF
ALL THE WORRIES AND
CARES OF THE WORLD,
AND JUST CURL UP
INTO A BALL
AND **SLEEP**.

115

INNER **PEACE**

IS

BUT ONE

OUTCOME

OF STILLNESS.

"THE REST

IS

SILENCE."

ACKNOWLEDGMENTS

Cat People Extraordinaire:

Thanks to my wise and wonderful literary agent, Kimberley Cameron, for knowing just where to find the perfect home for Guru Zuzu.

Many thanks to all the singularly nice people at New World Library who took Guru Zuzu into their hearts. My especial thanks to my editorial director, the ever-gracious, always-insightful Georgia Hughes; to my very talented art director, Tracy Cunningham; and to Kristen Cashman, who proved to be a managing editor of rare perspicacity.

Thanks also to Dr. Bill Estheimer, DVM, of San Rafael, California, for all the kindness and care he gave to Zuzu.

Lastly, eternal thanks to my wife, Christine, for rescuing Zuzu and bringing her home and into our lives. We learned we were to be the little black Bombay pussycat's third "guardians"; and never has "third time's a charm" proved more true or such a blessing.

Cats Extraordinaire:

Thanks to Mimi and Coco who remind me every day just how much there is still to be learned from the wisdom of cats.

ILLUSTRATION CREDITS

P. 17:
Cat in Cooking Pot | Juan Martin
Creative Commons | AnimalsClipArt.com

P. 19:
Stalking Cat | Théophile-Alexandre Steinlen
Dover Pictorial Archive

P. 21:
Cat and Mouse | Russell Coulson
CoulsonCollection.com

P. 23:
Cat and Mies | Tony Broadbent
Coco on MR10 cantilever chair designed by Mies van der Rohe

P. 25:
Caterwauling Cat | Tony Broadbent
Inspired by antique hand-painted wall-sign

P. 27:
Mimi the Sphinx | Tony Broadbent
Inspired by a love of Ancient Egypt and Mimi's love of striking the perfect pose

P. 29:
Kitteh Dangerous | **Rones**
Creative Commons | OpenClipArt.org

P. 33:
Coco the Clown Celebrating Red Nose Day
Tony Broadbent

I·AM·A·CAT

P. 37:
Very Wise Japanese Cat | **Artist unknown**
From the cover of *I Am Not a Cat* by Natsumi
Sōseki (1909) | Public domain

P. 31:
Cat and Avenue of Trees | **Artist unknown**
From *The Writings in Prose and Verse of Rudyard
Kipling* (1897) | Firkin | Creative Commons
OpenClipArt.org

P. 35:
Cat in Treetop
Russell Coulson & Tony Broadbent

P. 39:
Mimi the Kitten | **Tony Broadbent**
*7-month-old Mimi explaining her preferred routine
to me…yet again*

P. 43:
Cat and Rubies | Russell Coulson
CoulsonCollection.com

P. 45:
Love Is a Two-Way Street | Tony Broadbent

P. 47:
Catnap | Russell Coulson
CoulsonCollection.com

P. 49:
Cat Food for Thought | David Sopp
WryBaby.com

```
>   /\,,,,/ \
>   ( =';'= )
>   /*??*\
>  (.|.|..|.|.)
```

P. 51:
Keyboard Kat | Tony Broadbent
Coco and Mimi typed this all by themselves

P. 53:
The Uncommon Cat | William Nicholson
From *The Square Book of Animals* (1900)
Public domain

P. 55:
Leaping Cat | Russell Gray
Creative Commons | AnimalsClipArt.com

P. 57:
Schrödinger's Cat | Tony Broadbent
Inspired by classic horror-film poster

P. 59:
Cat Burglar Cat | Russell Coulson
CoulsonCollection.com

P. 61:
I Want to Be Alone Cat | Artist unknown
Public domain | Clipart by KissCC0.com

P. 63:
Black Cats and Red Cherries | Tony Broadbent
Inspired by cats Bill and Ben from a photo by
Joe Broadbent

P. 65:
Heart of Cats | Artist unknown
Creative Commons | OpenClipArt.org

123

P. 69:
Best Friend Forever Cat | Russell Coulson
CoulsonCollection.com

P. 71:
Coco Bean | Tony Broadbent

P. 73:
Mom Asleep with Kitten
Théophile-Alexandre Steinlen
Dover Pictorial Archive

P. 75:
Poe's Tonsorial Black Cat with Bats
Russell Coulson
CoulsonCollection.com

P. 77:
Countless Coco Beans | Tony Broadbent

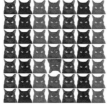

P. 79:
Cat and Computer Mouse | Russell Coulson
CoulsonCollection.com

P. 81:
"This Is Not a Pipe" | Artist unknown
Communist-era Czechoslovakia matchbox cover

P. 83:
Dancing Cats | David Sopp
WryBaby.com

P. 85:
Fish Bone Smiley Cat | Tony Broadbent

P. 87:
The Three Tenors Caterwaul | Russell Coulson
CoulsonCollection.com

P. 89:
Coco Bean and Her Bunny
Tony Broadbent

P. 91:
Ha Ha Felix the Cat
Pat Sullivan & Otto Messmer
Film still from *Felix in Hollywood* (1923)
Public domain

P. 95:
The Cat's Meow! | Tony Broadbent

P. 97:
Cat and Mouse Hole | Russell Coulson
CoulsonCollection.com

P. 99:
Cat on Skateboard | Russell Coulson
CoulsonCollection.com

P. 101:
Cats at Play | Russell Coulson
CoulsonCollection.com

P. 103:
Scary Black Cat with Bats | Russell Coulson
CoulsonCollection.com

P. 105:
The Thinker Cat | David Sopp
WryBaby.com

P. 107:
Cat Descending
Théophile-Alexandre Steinlen
Dover Pictorial Archive

P. 109:
Traversée de Chats | Spadassin
Creative Commons | OpenClipArt.org

P. 111:
Cat at Dinner | Russell Coulson
CoulsonCollection.com

P. 113:
Hommage à Théophile-Alexandre Steinlen
Russell Coulson | CoulsonCollection.com

P. 115:
Sleeping Cat | Théophile-Alexandre Steinlen
Dover Pictorial Archive

P. 117:
Om Cat | Tony Broadbent
Inspired by the music of George Harrison

127

ABOUT THE **ILLUSTRATORS** AND **PHOTOGRAPHERS**

Cover: Ruslan Olinchuk. Photographer and designer. To my eye, Ruslan's simple but brilliantly accomplished creation captures the true essence of "feline wisdom." It's certainly a worthy simulacrum of dear departed Guru Zuzu. And, yes, the allusion to the immortal sage Yoda may be entirely coincidental but is wonderfully appropriate.
Photo: Colourbox.com

Pages 19, 73, 107, 115: Théophile-Alexandre Steinlen (1859–1923). Born in Lausanne, Switzerland. The master — one of the greatest illustrators, painters, printmakers, and sculptors of Belle Époque Paris. His cat studies are wonderfully observed; his beautiful line, timeless. From *Cats: Wordless Picture-Stories* and *Cats and Other Animals*. Thanks to Dover Pictorial Archive for gathering together so many fine examples in *Steinlen's Cats*, four of which are included in this book. (The illustration on page 113 is Russell Coulson's homage to "the master.")

Pages 21, 35, 43, 47, 59, 69, 75, 79, 87, 97, 99, 101, 103, 111, 113: Russell Coulson. Illustrator and fine artist. Russell lives in the UK and is a dear, dear friend whom I've known and worked with for many years. His work is wide-ranging and astonishingly prolific — in painting and drawing style, as well as subject matter. He's forever been in search of the ever-elusive "line." There have been numerous exhibitions of his work in the UK and Australia. You can see more at CoulsonCollection.com.

Pages 49, 83, 105: David Sopp. Art director, graphic designer, illustrator, humorist, and cofounder of Wry Baby. Another extremely talented friend I've known and worked with for many years. You can see more of his many works at WryBaby.com

Pages 10, 23, 25, 27, 33, 35, 39, 45, 51, 57, 63, 71, 77, 85, 89, 95, 117, 132, 133: Tony Broadbent. Designer and illustrator. Photographs of different generations of black cats — Zuzu, Mimi, and Coco — were taken on different generations of iPhone. Whatever did we do "to catch the moment" before cameras in smartphones?

Page 135: Picture of Zuzu by great photographer and friend **Curt Fischer**.

I also wish to acknowledge and give thanks to the artists whose works in the public domain appear in this book: **William Nicholson** (p. 53), **Pat Sullivan** (p. 91), **Otto Messmer** (p. 91). And to those illustrators and designers whose Creative Commons works also appear in this book: **Juan Martin** (p. 17), **Rones** (p. 29), **Firkin** (p. 31), **Russell Gray** (p. 55), and **Spadassin** (p. 109).

ABOUT **TONY BROADBENT**

Tony Broadbent is an award-winning author, writer, designer, illustrator, speaker, and noted authority on The Beatles. He's written for newspapers, magazines, radio, television, and film. He's the author of the *In the Smoke* series of mystery novels about a cat burglar in postwar London; as well as *The One After 9:09: A Mystery with a Backbeat* — a novel about the early years of The Beatles; and a history: *The Beatles in Liverpool, Hamburg, and London*. He is a contributing editor of the Facebook blog *Beatles Forever*. His work has also appeared in the short story anthologies *Mystery Writers of America Presents: The Mystery Box* and *A Study in Sherlock: Stories Inspired by the Holmes Canon*.

Tony Broadbent was born in Windsor, England. He now lives and works in the San Francisco Bay Area. Word is that cats have ever loomed large in his life.

COCO

MIMI

ZUZU

NEW WORLD LIBRARY is dedicated to publishing books and other media that inspire and challenge us to improve the quality of our lives and the world.

We are a socially and environmentally aware company. We recognize that we have an ethical responsibility to our readers, our authors, our staff members, and our planet.

We serve our readers by creating the finest publications possible on personal growth, creativity, spirituality, wellness, and other areas of emerging importance. We serve our authors by working with them to produce and promote quality books that reach a wide audience. We serve New World Library employees with generous benefits, significant profit sharing, and constant encouragement to pursue their most expansive dreams.

Whenever possible, we print our books with soy-based ink on 100 percent postconsumer-waste recycled paper. We power our offices with solar energy and contribute to nonprofit organizations working to make the world a better place for us all.

Our products are available wherever books are sold. Visit our website to download our catalog, subscribe to our e-newsletter, read our blog, and link to authors' websites, videos, and podcasts.

customerservice@newworldlibrary.com
Phone: 415-884-2100 or 800-972-6657
Orders: Ext. 10 · Catalog requests: Ext. 10
Fax: 415-884-2199

www.newworldlibrary.com